This book belongs to

_____

Hostess Extraordinaire

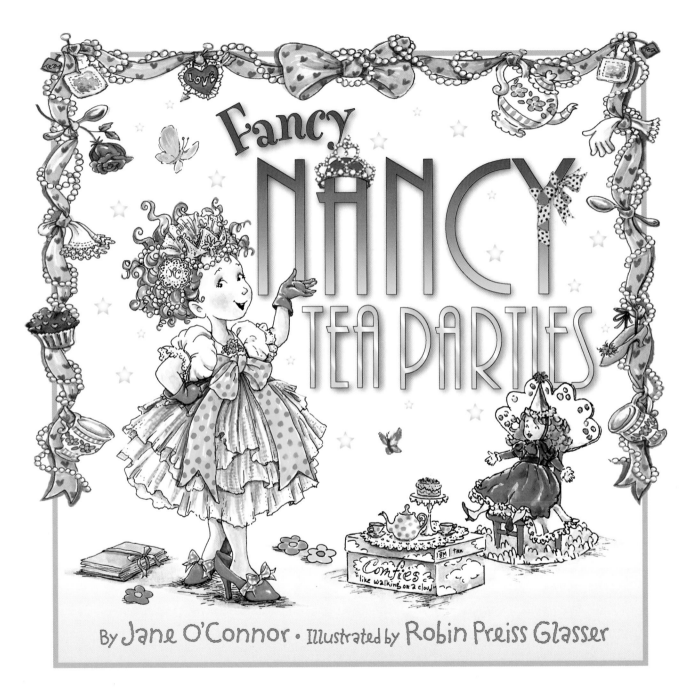

Fancy NANCY TEA PARTIES

By Jane O'Connor • Illustrated by Robin Preiss Glasser

HARPER

An Imprint of HarperCollinsPublishers

For Aunt Rocky, hostess extraordinaire, whose
"Nothing Special String Beans" are a prized recipe in our family
—J. O'C.

For my grandmother Lillian Splaver, who would have adored Nancy
—R.P.G.

Fancy Nancy: Tea Parties
Text copyright © 2009 by Jane O'Connor
Illustrations copyright © 2006, 2007, 2008, 2009 by Robin Preiss Glasser
Printed in the U.S.A. All rights reserved.

Library of Congress Cataloging-in-Publication Data
O'Connor, Jane.
    Fancy Nancy: tea parties / written by Jane O'Connor ; illustrated by Robin Preiss
Glasser. — 1st ed.
        p.   cm.
    Summary: In her own inimitable style, the girl who loves to use fancy words provides
tips on how to host the perfect tea party, describing how to behave, food and drinks to serve,
games to play, and much more.
    ISBN 978-0-06-200300-3
    [1. Tea—Fiction.   2. Parties—Fiction.   3. Vocabulary—Fiction]   I. Preiss-Glasser,
Robin, ill.   II. Title.
PZ7.O222Fgl 2009   2008051776
[E]—dc22   CIP
                                                                            AC

Typography by Jeanne L. Hogle
10 11 12 13 14 COM 05 04 03 02 01
❖
First Edition

Bonjour, everybody!

What I love most about tea parties is that you can have one anytime! You don't need to wait for your birthday or Christmas or some other formal occasion (that's a fancy way of saying an important day). Whenever you feel like celebrating, that's the perfect time for a tea party. (I often feel like celebrating.)

I have been the hostess of so many tea parties that I am practically an expert about what to wear, which refreshments to serve, and how to make everything look *très* elegant.

There are just three important things to remember:

-  Be fancy!
- Have fun.
- Don't forget to invite me!

Divinely yours,
Nancy

TABLE OF CONTENTS

ENSEMBLES

(Ensembles is fancy for outfits.)

You can really wear anything to a tea party—as long as it's fancy.

If guests arrive looking too casual (that's a polite way of saying plain), no problem! I always have lots of accessories on hand.

Beads

Baubles

Hair Stuff

Magic 4 Kids

Bag o' Bows

X-mas ornaments

ETIQUETTE

(Etiquette is French for polite manners.)

Here are some things to remember—besides saying "please" and "thank you," of course!

🏆 If you burp, put your hand over your mouth and say, **"Excusez-moi!"**

🏆 Your napkin belongs in your lap, not on your head.

🏆 Try not to grab.

🏆 Compliment your hostess. That means saying nice things like **"This is yummy."**

CLASSIC TEA PARTIES

Classic tea parties are where guests sit at a pretty table. Mrs. DeVine and I pretend to be famous and call each other "darling."

Nancy's French Words

Merci	mare-see	thank you
Non	nawh	no
De rien	duh ree-uh	you're welcome
S'il vous plaît	see voo play	please
Excusez-moi	ekks-kyoo-zay mwah	excuse me
Oui	wee	yes
Très	tray	very

At tea parties, it's fun to speak French as much as possible.

I keep cards with French words in a fancy box.

"Excusez-moi" —ekks-kyoo-zay-mwah
excuse me

"S'il vous plaît" —see voo play
please

"Merci" —mare-see
thank you

"Magnifique" —manny-feek
magnificent

"De rien" —duh ree-uh
you're welcome

You look magnifique!

Merci, darling!

5

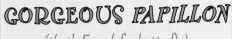

GORGEOUS *PAPILLON*
(that's French for butterfly)
PLACE MATS

Fold a piece of construction paper in half.

Fold ↘

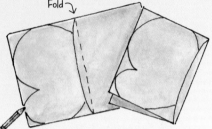

Draw the same shape I have. Cut it out and open it.

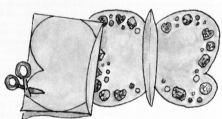

Add jewel stickers around the edges. *Voilà!* You're done.

When I'm planning a tea party, my best friend, Bree, often assists me (that's fancy for helps out). Sometimes I borrow Bree's fancy china set. But often we just use plain paper plates.

Put doilies on paper plates and—*voilà*—they're fancy.

Using cloth napkins is very fancy, and so is dabbing your lips with them.

The napkins don't all need to be the same. Mix-and-match them. It will look so stylish, which means fancy in a very interesting way.

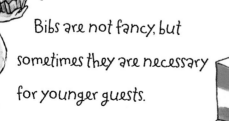

Bibs are not fancy, but sometimes they are necessary for younger guests.

CAN PAPER NAPKINS LOOK FANCY?

Oui, oui, oui, when you fold them into fans.

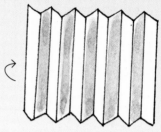

Take the napkin and make tiny accordion folds.

Fold over one end.

Place the napkin in a cup and open the fan. *TRÈS FAN-CY.*

I use plastic flatware at all my parties. (Flatware is a fancy word for spoons and forks and knives.) Sometimes I put one or two jewel stickers on the handles. Or I take a permanent marker and monogram them. That means I write my initials, which are NC for Nancy Clancy.

Place cards are tiny signs that tell your guests where to sit. Sometimes I take lollipops and tape a name on each. Then I stick each lollipop into a marshmallow.

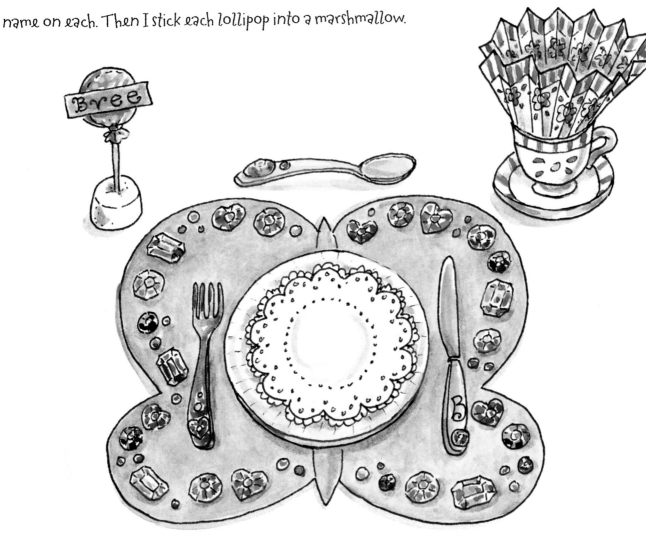

Here is a finished place setting that I'm sure you'll agree looks very elegant.

BEVERAGES

(That's a fancy word for drinks.)

Do you need to serve tea at a tea party? No. But this recipe for iced tea is delicious (that's fancy for yummy). You need to make it the day before with help from a grown-up. So ask nicely, s'il vous plaît.

Sunshine Tea à la Nancy

Place four to six tea bags in a pitcher and fill it with two quarts of water. Cover the pitcher so that nothing can get inside. Place the pitcher outside in sunlight and leave it there for three to five hours. (As the sun moves, make sure to move your pitcher too!) Then put the pitcher in the refrigerator. Before you serve the iced tea, add sugar. A little orange juice in it is very tasty too.

Extra-fancy Fuchsia Lemonade

Make a can of pink lemonade, then add cranberry juice to make it hot pink. (You can also put in some raspberries or blueberries if you have them.)

REFRESHMENTS

(That's a fancy word for snacks.)

You can never go wrong serving tea sandwiches at a tea party. Do they actually have tea in them? *Non!* Remember to eat them with pinkies up!

Nancy's Nibblers

(I like to give all my recipes fancy names!)

Spread cream cheese on slices of date bread. Then put raisin or banana slices on top. Cut each slice into four triangles. You don't need a top slice. Keeping them open-faced looks fancier.

Raspberry Swirls

Cut the crust off a slice of white bread and place it between two pieces of waxed paper. Flatten it out with a rolling pin. Now spread raspberry jam—or any flavor you like—on the bread and roll it into a log. Cut the log into slices. Don't they look pretty?

A hostess never wants her guests to be sick, so make sure nobody is allergic to the refreshments you serve.

RECREATION

(That's fancy for games.)

At tea parties, my guests sometimes like to play games. Here's a fun one.

Packing for Paris

This is a memory game. The first guest says, "I'm packing for Paris and I'm taking a boa."

The next guest repeats that and adds another accessory.

"I'm packing for Paris and I'm taking a boa and a *tiara*."

The next guest adds a third accessory to the list.

Keep going around the table.

You must remember everything in order.

If you goof, you're out.

I'll go first. I'm packing for Paris and I'm taking a boa.

I'm packing for Paris and I'm taking a boa and a tiara.

I'm packing for Paris and I'm taking a boa, a tiara, and a baseball hat.

11

BUFFET TEA PARTIES

Buffet is a fancy word for a party where guests serve themselves. If you invite lots of friends and don't have enough chairs, a buffet tea party is the perfect answer (a fancier word is solution!). After guests take their food, they sit wherever they want. I also encourage guests to mix and mingle.

CENTERPIECES

For a buffet, everything is set out on a big table.

I always have a beautiful centerpiece to decorate it.

Lollipop Bouquet

(Bouquet is a French word that means a bunch of flowers.)

Fill a flowerpot with jelly beans. Stick in lollipops—all different flavors and sizes. If you want, you can tape paper petals to the lollipops.

Blossoms Extravaganza

Often Mrs. DeVine lets me pick wildflowers from her garden. Then I put them in a teapot.

Gorgeous!

Wrapping flatware and napkins for your guests mak[es]
it more convenient (that's fancy for easy and helpful).

Sometimes I write each guest's name on a ribbon. Then I tie the
ribbon around the napkin with the flatware inside.

If I have more time, Bree helps me make paper flowers with pipe-cleaner stems
that we wrap around the napkins. (Bree is much better at this than I am.)

TISSUE-PAPER FLOWER

Cut a few pieces of
tissue paper into squares.

Put them in a pile and
fold it like an accordion.

Tie the center with a green pipe
cleaner and then gently pull each piece
of paper apart into a flower shape.

After your guests are finished eating, they can put the
flowers on their wrists. Ooh la la! It's a corsage.
(That's French for a small bouquet that you wear.)

REFRESHMENTS

At buffets, it's best to serve food

that won't fall off your plate if it's on your lap.

Crunchy Munchy Crudités

(croo-dee-tay)

Crudités are raw vegetables. (Doesn't it sound much fancier in French?) Ask a grown-up to help you cut carrot sticks and little broccoli trees. Snow-pea pods are also good. Arrange them on a platter.

Mademoiselle Clancy's Honey Dip

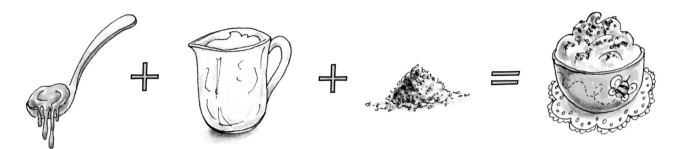

Mix a tablespoon of honey into a cup of plain yogurt.
Sprinkle a little brown sugar on top. Tasty!

Delectable Fruit Kebabs

(Delectable is fancy for yummy.)

Put strawberries, banana slices, grapes, and blueberries
on frilly toothpicks. (Don't you think frilly toothpicks
make everything taste better?) Dip the kebabs in the
honey dip—dee-lish.

(Don't worry if you don't have frilly toothpicks.
You can make a toothpick fancy by sticking a mini-
marshmallow or a gumdrop on one end.)

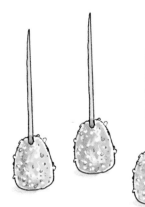

Jus de Pomme

(zhoo duh pumm)

This is apple juice, but saying it in French makes it automatically fancy.

ORANGE FIZZEROO

Pour two cups of orange juice into a pitcher.

Add half a cup of sparkling water

and half a cup of orange or lemon sherbet.

Very refreshing!

Follow the Hostess

Here's another game. Everybody gets in a line behind the hostess. Whatever the hostess does—like skipping, hopping, crawling, or walking on tippy toes—everybody else has to do too. The hostess should switch from one thing to another lots of times. There's no winner. It's just silly and fun to play.

TEA PARTIES ALFRESCO

(That's Italian for outdoors.)

On beautiful days, there's absolutely no reason why a tea party has to be inside.

Turn the page for a surprise.

On the menu board:

Menu:
✿ Strawberries Supreme ✿
✿ Festive Fondue Parfaits

Ooh la la! Our picnic table is so much fancier now, don't you agree?

When tea parties are outside, my parents don't mind if we serve refreshments that are a little messy.

Strawberries Supreme
(Supreme is fancy for the best.)

All you need is a bowl of strawberries, a bowl of instant whipped cream, and a bowl of sprinkles. Dip a strawberry into the whipped cream and then top with some sprinkles.

Festive Fondue (fon-doo)

Fondue is French for a dipping sauce with pieces of bread or fruit. It's *très* simple. Place a bowl of chocolate sauce on a plate and surround it with fruit on frilly toothpicks.

Now dip away.

And now, for the ultimate gourmet treat, turn the page.

It's Parfait Time!

A parfait, as you may already know,
is French for ice-cream sundae.

Put out different flavors of ice cream

as well as
chocolate sauce,

instant whipped cream,

banana slices,

strawberries,

and sprinkles.

Then guests each take a bowl and create their own parfait.

Fancy Freeze Tag

Here's the way my friends and I play it. The last person to say "Not it" is "It." If you're It, you chase everybody around. When you tag them they have to freeze in a fancy pose. They can be unfrozen if somebody else runs by and touches them, shouting, "*Voilà*, you're unfrozen." We usually play until we get bored or exhausted—that's fancy for tired!

TEA FOR TWO

The copresidents of the Explorer Extraordinaire Club
(Bree and me) often hold tea parties in our clubhouse.
Because the club is about exploring in the wild,
sometimes we give our parties a nature theme.

Ants on a Log

Have a grown-up help you cut celery sticks. Spread cream cheese inside each "log" and then top with "ants" (raisins).

Ladybug Cookies

Put a little red food coloring into a dish of vanilla frosting. Mix with a spoon until it is red. Spread on round cookies as shown and top with chocolate bits. *Très adorable.*

DOLL TEA PARTIES

Can you guess who likes tea parties even more than
I do? My doll Marabelle. Her full name is Marabelle
Lavinia Chandelier.

   Her best friend is Sarinda, who is a lovely person,
although not fancy at all.

   Her other best friend is a pink puppy named Sequin.

   Poor Frenchy! She would love to come to these tea
parties. But often the refreshments—especially anything
with chocolate—would make her sick.

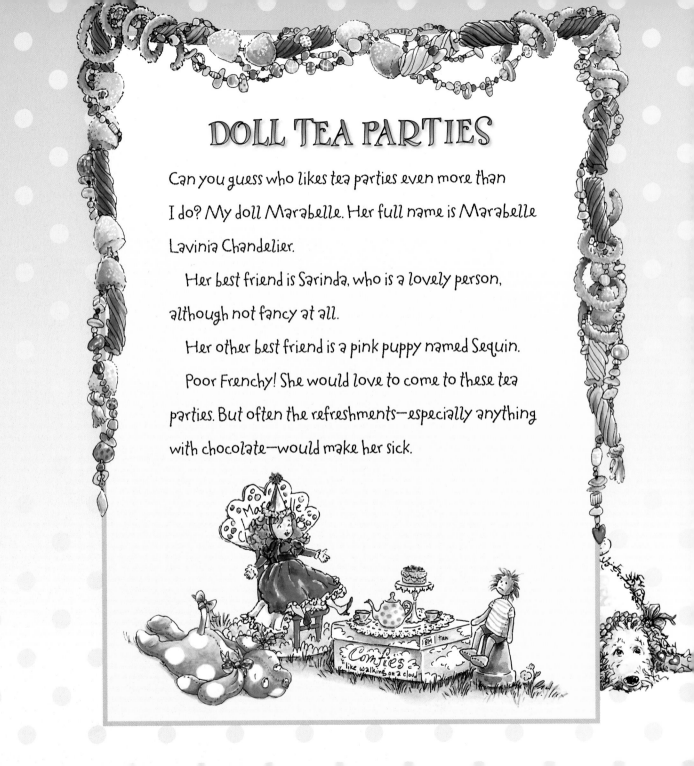

A shoe box makes an excellent table. And a cloth napkin, doily, or hankie can be used as a lovely tablecloth.

Shells make beautiful bowls. I put Cheerios in them. And I save old toothpaste caps for doll's cups.

For place mats, little cotton pads (the kind for taking off nail polish) work very nicely, especially when you add on a few jewel stickers.

Smear frosting on cookies—*voilà*, it's a doll-sized cake. (If Marabelle and her guests aren't hungry, then I eat it!)

CONCLUSION

(That's fancy for the end.)

Every hostess has special treats that she serves at her tea parties. Since it is important to remember exactly how to make them, I keep a recipe card for each one.

Here are some recipe cards for you that are just like the ones I use. If you like, keep them in an index-card box decorated with jewel stickers. On the top of the box, write your monogram in glitter.

Party on!